Emma's Gift

Molly Schaar Idle

Abingdon Press
Nashville

Emma's Gift

Scripture quotation is from the New Revised Standard Version of the Bible.
Copyright © 1989 by the Division of Christian Education of the National Council of Churches of Christ in the U.S.A.
Used by permission

0-687-02294-0

04 05 06 07 08 09 10 11 12 — 10 9 8 7 6 5 4 3
Printed in China

It hadn't snowed in over two weeks, and now it was Christmas Eve, and Emma was worried that there wouldn't be any snow for Christmas morning. She stared out the front window and hoped that if she stared hard enough that maybe she could make just a few flakes fall from the sky.

No luck.

"Gee," thought Emma. "This is the worst!"
In the kitchen, the phone rang. Emma ignored it and continued her
vigil by the window. A few moments later Emma's mom came in
from the kitchen.

"That was Manna on the phone," she said. "I'm afraid that it is snowing so hard at the airport that her plane can't take off, and she won't be here for Christmas morning."

"What?!" yelped Emma. "First no snow, and now, no Manna! Christmas isn't Christmas without them!" She slumped into a chair by the fireplace.

"I know," said Mom, "but to help make it up to you, she said you can open her present early."

Emma's face lit up, and in a flash she was underneath the tree in search of Manna's package. She found it,

weighed it,

gave it a little shake,

and then in a flurry of ribbons and paper,

she unwrapped it.

Under the layers of tissue Emma found a rainbow-colored scarf, matching mittens, and a brand new pair of shiny red galoshes. There was also a note. It said,
"To my sweet Emma—
To keep you warm in the snow while we build our Christmas tradition.
Love, Manna."

Every year Emma and Manna got up early on Christmas morning and built a terrific snowman. Each one they made was bigger and better than the last! This year, thought Emma, there would be no snowman, and no Manna. She held the package to her chest and stared out of the window again, still no snow.

Later as Mom tucked her into bed,
Emma wore the scarf and mittens to remind her of Manna.

Mom made her take off the galoshes.

Then Emma drifted off to sleep dreaming of snowmen.

In the morning she woke up, slipped on her galoshes over her sneakers, and sprinted downstairs to see if Santa had come—and he had! Stockings were stuffed, and she got everything she wanted except . . .

She sighed and looked out the window. There was still no snow and worst of all, no Manna.

THANK YOU!

S.C.

After all of the gifts had been opened, Emma's mom asked her to go down to the town square and pick up their Christmas wreath while she made breakfast. Emma, bundled up in her gifts from Manna, and with money in her hand, set off down the street.

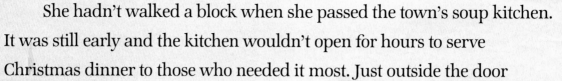

She hadn't walked a block when she passed the town's soup kitchen. It was still early and the kitchen wouldn't open for hours to serve Christmas dinner to those who needed it most. Just outside the door Emma could see a thin little man in the doorway. His clothes were worn, he carried a small knapsack, and he was blowing hard on his hands to try and keep them warm.

Emma looked at her own hands, all toasty and warm inside
the mittens that Manna had sent. She looked at the thin little man
again, and took off her mittens.

She knew she shouldn't speak to strangers, and so she wondered how she might give the mittens to the man without being seen. Just then a truck pulled up to the curb and the driver called to the thin little man to ask for directions. He placed his knapsack on the ground and walked over to the truck. Emma crept up to the knapsack, placed her mittens from Manna on top, and was off before the man turned back.

From around the corner, Emma could see the look of delight on the man's face as he saw the mittens and slipped them on his hands.

"Merry Christmas," she whispered. Then she smiled to herself, pushed her hands deep in her pockets to keep warm, and headed off down the street.

As she passed a small walkway between two buildings, she heard a funny scratching sound, followed by a tiny meow. As Emma listened, she realized that the sound was coming from a barrel placed under a pipe to catch rainwater.

Emma looked down into the barrel; and to her surprise, she saw a shivering kitten

stuck at the bottom!

She tried to stick her arm in to rescue him but couldn't quite reach. She had an idea!

First, Emma unwrapped the scarf that Manna had given her from around her neck.

Then, she dangled it into the barrel, and the little kitten grabbed hold.

As she pulled him up and wrapped his shivering body in the scarf, she heard a woman's voice.

"Tabby," the woman called out. "Tabby, where are you?" Emma, bundled the kitten in her arms and turned around. The woman was dressed in her bathrobe and standing on the steps of her house, calling out toward the street. The kitten let out another meow. The woman spun around, clapped her hands together in delight, and let out a gasp of surprise and relief.

"Tabby," she cried. "I thought I'd lost you!" She rushed over to Emma, and scooped the little kitten, scarf and all, into her arms. The woman beamed at her. "Thank you so much for saving Tabby! I live by myself, and he is the only family I have. I don't know what I would have done if you hadn't found him for me."

Emma gave the kitten a pat on the head, and tucked the scarf Manna had given her under his little kitten chin.

"Merry Christmas," said the woman as she turned back up the stairs. "Merry Christmas," said Emma. Then she turned up the collar of her coat and put her hands deep in her pockets to keep warm as she headed down the street.

Finally, she reached the
Christmas wreath stand in the
town square. Standing there,
selling wreaths, was a boy
younger than Emma.

She reached out to give the boy her money in exchange for the wreath, but a quarter slipped out of her hand and fell onto the sidewalk. When she bent down to pick it up, Emma noticed that the boy had a big hole in one of his sneakers. The boy, ashamed, hid one shoe behind the other.

"Why don't your parents get you a new pair of shoes?" asked Emma looking up at him.

"Dad got hurt and lost his job," said the boy. "My mom is selling Christmas wreaths to help us get by." Then he added proudly, "I'm minding the stand a minute while she's inside checking on Dad."

"Oh," said Emma, embarrassed that she had asked, and stared down at her feet.

She looked at the last thing that Manna had given her, the shiny red galoshes that fit just right. She thought hard and bit her lip.

"You know," said Emma, "these galoshes are much too tight on me, but I bet they would fit you just right."

The boy looked questioningly at her. "But you don't even know me, why would you give me your galoshes?"

"Just think of it as a Christmas present," said Emma smiling, as she slipped the galoshes off and handed them to the boy.

"I don't know how to thank you," whispered the boy, as he held the shiny red galoshes lovingly in his hands.

"Put them on," urged Emma, and as he did his face lit up.

"Merry Christmas," grinned the boy.

"Merry Christmas," said Emma as she handed the boy the quarter and took the wreath from his hand.

Then she stomped her feet, turned up the collar of her coat, and put her hands deep in her pockets to keep warm, as she crossed the town square toward the bus stop to go home.

As she walked, a bus came down the street to the town square and made a stop. When it pulled away, Emma saw an older woman standing at the bus stop. Emma looked. She looked again.

"Manna!" she cried out as she ran across the square.

Manna opened up her arms and swept Emma off her feet and hugged her, and hugged her, and hugged her some more.

"How did you get here?" asked Emma.

"Well," said Manna, "I couldn't miss Christmas with my sweet Emma, and since I couldn't fly, I took the all night bus instead! But where are your gifts?" she asked looking at Emma. "Didn't your Mom tell you to open them early?"

Emma stared down at her feet where the shiny red galoshes used to be and gulped.

"Manna, I gave them away," she said guiltily.

"Gave them away?" asked Manna. "Didn't you like them?"

"Oh yes, Manna, I loved them but . . ."

As they walked home Emma told her all about the thin little man at the soup kitchen, and Tabby the lost kitten, and the boy at the Christmas wreath stand with the hole in his sneaker. Manna listened, and when Emma had finished, and they had reached the front door she said,

"Emma, I am so proud of you."

"Proud?" asked Emma. "I gave away your gifts."

"But you are the greatest gift of all," said Manna.

And as they hugged each other, Emma felt warmer than she ever had with the mittens, or the scarf, or the shiny red galoshes.

Just then, it started to snow.

Give and it will be given to you. A good measure, pressed down, shaken together, running over, will be put into your lap; for the measure you give will be the measure you get back.

Luke 6:38

Madison